For Daddy,
the happiest person I know

- Rachel -

A TEMPLAR BOOK

First published in the UK in 2012 by Templar Publishing,
an imprint of The Templar Company Limited,
The Granary, North Street, Dorking, Surrey, RH4 1DN, UK
www.templarco.co.uk

ISBN 978-1-84877-636-4

Printed in the U.K.

A Handful of Happiness

Lovely little mini-wisdoms on LIFE from the bright side

Wonderful you... repeat after me...

The HAPPY Mantra

 Today I will be a BIG bundle of HAPPINESS.

A one-person loVe train to Smiley town.

In fact...
I will not only be happy myself
but I will ripple happiness
ripple
ripple

through the World,
by being really Very lovely to everyone.*

*Even grumpy people.

If I ever begin to feel

less happy

I will immediately think of my
FAVOURITE PEOPLE
& my FAVOURITE THINGS
(like lying on the grass on a sunny day or puppies
or hearing someone belly-laugh or doughnuts)

& instantly feel HAPPY again.

I might also say this little thing in my head:

I am Wonderful.
I am wonderful.
I am amazing.
The World is a GIANT playground
& I am going to play in it.

Yes I am.

Yes... repeat after me...

I will also learn COOL FACTS &
then tell them to people with my

eyebrows   raised

& wait for
them to be

MAJORLY IMPRESSED
that I know them.

Because that is very happifying indeed.

Yes...

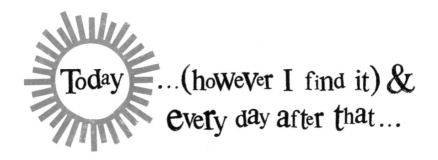
Today ...(however I find it) & every day after that...

I will be that person,
the One everyone says,

"Oh, them?
The happy one?"

And that will be me.

It will.

Always remember this happy thought...

YOUR BODY is merely the FROSTING on the TRUE Cake of your SOULy Bit*.

*But
what
mighty
fine
frosting
it is.

& Whatever you do...

Don't Tip-toe around the PUddles of Life.... Wade through tHe River of Destiny.*

If you are feeling IMPATIENT, apply immediate:

CAKE & other ways

There are some things in life it is impossible not to feel happy about whilst partaking of them. In fact these happy things are EVERYWHERE if you look closely enough. Here are twelve* of the many speedy ways to INSTANT happiness heaven:

*There are at least twelthty zillion others, but this is a nice number to start with.

1. Cake

2. The Sun on your face
(or other bodily bits)

3. Listening to Barry White Songs

4. CAKE

5. Creating & then showcasing
an innovative dance move

to InStant Happiness

6. Paying someone a compliment

7. Playing something your life doesn't depend on as if your life depends on it (like frisbee or tiddlywink or scrabble)

8. CAKE

9. Learning a new fact

10. Stroking a kitten (puppies are also excellent)

11. Punching the air with your eyes shut

12. CAAAAAKE

Oh yes... if you do these things...

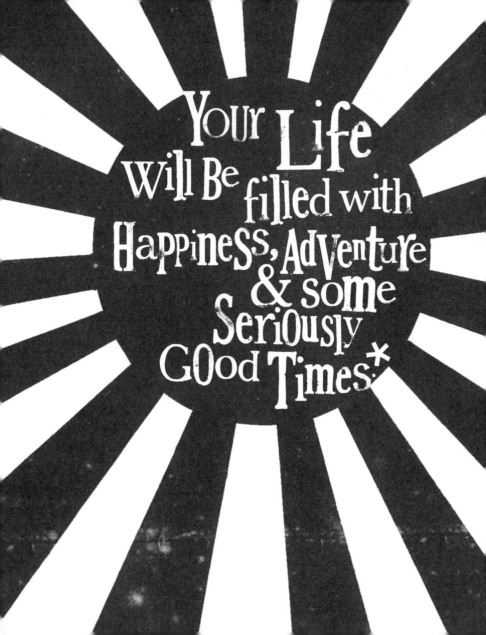

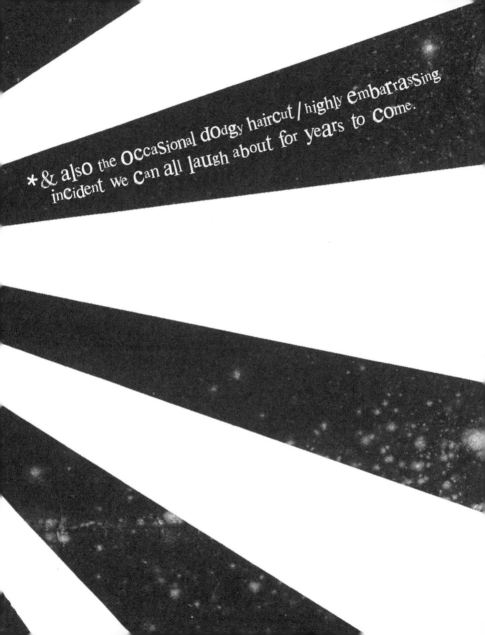

* & also the occasional dodgy haircut / highly embarrassing incident we can all laugh about for years to come.

Try creating your own...

Happiness Manifesto

Give yourself three more presses
of the snooze button

Worry less

Snuggle at every possible Opportunity
(with & without Snuggle-ees)

Kick your health kick

Be nice

Stand up for someone
(or Something)

Make your mum proud

Take a deep breath

Bobble hat it up

(But don't wear your coat inside or you won't feel the benefit)

Champion porridge

Do something you've never done before

Surprise Someone

(extra points for surprising yourself)

Devote significant time
to Comfort food

Never take life too Seriously

& always look on the Bright side

Whenever in doubt, know that…

Everything Looks Better in the Morning.*

Every new dawn is full of promise if you...

Leap Out of bed & embrace the World of possibility that is the day ahead*

*Unless you are hungover, in which case DO NOT do ANY leaping & try to arrange for some fried food to be brought to you.

Know that True happiness is but a boiled egg away*

* If the egg is served by a Very good-looking person, in a bed, alongside an elaborate breakfast including Champagne, in an all-expenses-paid luxury Spa hotel offering Complimentary towelling robes.

Think
happy
thoughts*

*Occasional
rude ones
also
Okay.

Have
SunShine
in your
heart*.

*And
on your
White bits.

You see, there are TONS of teeny tiny yet terrifically

KiSs on the lips (ideally with prior permission).

Wear lots of colours (all in one go)

pOotle, potter, potter & prevaricate, procrastinate & pOntificate for a WHOLE peaceful & perfectly unproductive day.

Learn a new & inCredible fact (like that slugs have four noses or the average person laughs 10 times a day) & impress everyOne you know With it.

ReSurrect an Old joke.

tremendous tips to take you to the **TOP** of the World:

make Somebody else's day (& possibly night... you old fox, you).

Seek out baby animals & behold their cute-ness

Snuggle.

SING until your lungs (& somebody else's ears) hurt.

Crack Open some Bubbles (the drinking or blowing kind) for no particular reason.

And at times...

When you are at a difficult Crossroads in Life, take a Deep Breath & Stick the Kettle on*

*Unless you are at an actual crossroads, particularly in a car or something, when sticking a kettle on would be both dangerous & inappropriate.

Behold...

The Art of the FLIP SIDE

The Secret of TRUE HAPPINESS layeth here:

The Art of the flip Side

(The ninja-style ability to take any Situation – however
Seemingly bad – & flip it Sunny-side up).

The eXamples below are a Sort of... Warm-up.
The lunge before the Sprint, you might Say.

Flipsiding takes practice, but the force is Strong in you*
Practise So much you'd make even Mr Miyagi proud.

WaX on... WaX off...

Example Scenario 1: You have accidentally Shaved Off
One of your eyebrows. It lOoks pretty weird.

FLIP SIDE: This is fantastic! You've been
meaning to refresh your lOok for ageS.
GOODBYE MR CONVENTION,
have Some of that.

*You jedi-karate-kid-Warrior-jedi-thing, you

Example Scenario 2: You discover you've bought the winning lottery ticket! But a freak gust of wind blows it out of your hand & into the top branches of a tree, where it spontaneously combusts.

FLIP SIDE: What a lucky escape! This is the BEST thing that could have EVER happened to you. The money would have ruined you

(admit it, you'd have had a pool installed with your own face mosaic-ed on the bottom... I mean who wouldn't?)

as well as causing gargantuan rifts within your family & friends. Thank goodness none of THAT happened.

Example Scenario 3: You are jilted at the altar.

FLIP SIDE: Amazing! Thank goodness you found out about your fiancé's truly fickle nature just in time. Now you can bypass the boring speeches & get straight on to the party. Plus you'll probably meet a multi-millionaire model on your solo honeymoon & fall madly in love / lust. A narrow escape with a much happier ending.

And so, my friend, you have reached the end. But as a true flip-sider you will know it is also just the beginning... Go forth & be happy. Amazing One X